The Depth of the Riches

Burl L. Shepard

WORDS MATTER
PUBLISHING
OUR WORDS CHANGE THE WORLD

Words Matter Publishing
P.O. Box 531
Salem, Il 62881
www.wordsmatterpublishing.com

ISBN 13: 978-1-949809-99-2

Library of Congress Catalog Card Number: 2020919732

Table Of Contents

Part I The Upper Reaches.................................1
Part II The Great Valley..................................35
Part III The Visitor...75

Part I
The Upper Reaches

The man was awake. His eyes were closed, but he was aware. He was gathering his thoughts, trying to get a hold on the situation. He knew he was in a hospital room. He could see everything in his mind. Against the wall, on the left side of his bed, was a small, straight back chair, then the bathroom entrance door. Next was a small closet for hanging clothes and placing small items.

Beginning at the front wall, was the entrance door. An attached counter ran from the doorway the entire length of the wall. A computer sat on the counter along with medical equipment. Above the counter, a television was attached to the wall.

A window was on the right side, a heating and cooling unit underneath. A small shelf was between the window and the wall behind his bed. Around his bed was an array of machines and tubing. A table that could be pushed over the bed sat nearby. The bed was extremely comfortable. His body seemed to conform to it perfectly.

The man felt a slight breeze blowing across his body. The breeze carried the fragrance of blossoms and blooms.

Outside the window, the man heard the rustling of the tree foliage, then the chattering of a squirrel. So, it must be springtime, probably early morning, and the window had been raised. The only other sound was the chirping of birds. The man heard nothing mechanical, no sounds of vehicles, no sounds of men working. He thought that might be due to the early hour or that his room at the hospital might be located in a secluded location.

The man had a strange dream just before awakening. He dreamed a soft misty substance had fallen covering his entire body. The mist had caused a pleasant, tingling sensation, along with a feeling of well-being. The man had felt an excitement, an anxious readiness to start the new day.

Now, as he lie with eyes still closed, questions were flowing throughout his mind. The man knew he was in a hospital, but had no idea of its location, nor did he know what had transpired to cause him to be there. But most troubling, the man had no idea who he was. His identity was completely lost.

The man could remember different people frequently entering his room. Various doctors, nurses and attendants scurried about checking body functions, administering medications, and entering information into the computer that sat on the counter. Perhaps one of them would soon enter again. Or, when he opened his eyes, he might find someone sitting in the straight back chair, probably slumped in an uncomfortable position while trying to sleep. Then, he would be able to get answers, know what he was facing and what his future might hold. Hoping to soon ease his troubled mind, the man slowly opened his eyes, and in astonishment found himself looking into the clearest, bluest sky he had ever seen.

Stunned, he lie there trying to rationalize what had occurred. After the initial shock, he felt angry. Who could or would be so cruel to snatch a sick or injured person from a hospital room and place him in the outdoors alone and unprotected? How could a sick mind such as that exist?

For several moments the man lie still, then slowly turned his head to both sides. In wonderment, he saw a scattering of trees and bushes and the ground covered with lush, dark green grass. Many different colored flowers grew profusely throughout the landscape. The trees seemed to average twenty feet in height, the bushes four to six feet. A variety of strange-looking fruit grew on both trees and bushes in different sizes. Birds flew from bushes to trees as they enjoyed the abundant fruit. Butterflies flew about landing on bushes in bloom.

The man saw a squirrel scampering across the ground then jumping onto the side of a tree, pausing a moment before climbing to the mid-level branches where it methodically plucked and ate the bright colored fruit. What the man found most amazing were the colors he was seeing. He knew during his observation, he was seeing colors he had never seen before.

The man raised his head and looked down his body. He saw no bed covers and was surprised to find he was wearing dark brown walking shorts and a light brown, loose-fitting, button-down shirt. He frowned when he realized he was barefoot. While the landscape was beautiful, who could tell what lie hidden in the grass? A piece of tin or broken glass could cause serious, even life-threatening injury, especially if it was as it appeared—that no help would be available.

The man grabbed hold of both sides of his bed and discovered it was made of very hard, razor-thin material. He found this to be perplexing, as the bed had been very comfortable. He reached underneath the sides as far as he could from his position, but it remained the same. The man then pulled himself to a sitting position and immediately forgot the condition of his bed.

Before the man, there stretched a great valley. His current position seemed to be at the upper reaches of the valley. It was an expansive area, miles wide, the space before him extending farther than he could see. About thirty feet from where he sat, a rocky path led downward into the valley. The path curved left and was hidden by trees, bushes and boulders then curved back into sight and continued on its downward path. Both sides of the valley were bordered by uplands and hills. A large river coursed down the center with various streams, lakes and ponds on both sides. Grasslands, meadows and flat plains were scattered throughout.

Small, moving dots that appeared to be animals, moved about various areas within his vision range.

Suddenly, quite unexpectedly, the man's range of vision increased.

Incredibly, he was seeing many times normal as if he had somehow obtained zoom vision. The moving dots became herds of animals, and animals that roamed in packs and prides, and animals that roamed alone. There were many that should not be in the same geographical area. There were those not safe to be close to without protection or a barrier to keep them at bay.

As the man concentrated on the right side of the Great Valley, he focused on a large area of trees. Something within told him its expanse was great. It was truly a Big Forest within the Great Valley. As he was observing the trees, he caught movement. As the man watched a group of strange, man-like creatures walked single file along the edge of the Big Forest. He counted twelve. Their bodies were covered with greyish white-colored hair. They appeared to be extremely tall, especially the one leading. They had broad, muscular shoulders, narrow waists, and walked with athletic grace. Suddenly, the one leading the group veered into the forest followed by the others, and the man quickly lost sight of them. The man stared several moments at the trees, wondering if he had really seen the man-like creatures, but he knew he had. They were real.

As the man looked beyond the Big Forest and farther into the Great Valley, he realized what he was seeing as nothingness was actually water, and that from his vantage point he was looking at an extremely large area. The man was certain the large water at the far end of the Great Valley was very wide and very deep. Suddenly, as quickly as it had occurred, the zoom vision was gone. The man sat several moments, pondering all that he had seen. The most logical conclusion, he thought, was a dream. In fact, all that had happened was a dream. But no, the man knew reality, and everything that had occurred was very real, in fact, more real than anything he had ever experienced.

As the man became more oriented to his immediate surroundings, he became aware of another phenomenon. He realized he could see the ground beneath his bed. He then came to the remarkable conclusion the bed was transparent. He turned and sat on the side of the bed while carefully placing his feet onto the ground. The grass felt soft as velvet and covered the top of his toes. Slowly he stood, and with a shuffling motion carefully moved the sides of his feet through the grass in search of debris. Finding nothing in the soft grass, he turned toward the bed for a closer inspection. To the man's dismay, he found the bed not to be transparent as he had thought, but rather totally invisible.

The man felt the surface of the object, which by now he was considering to be more of a platform than a bed. The invisible platform had a hard-solid surface, which he thought was odd, for it had been very comfortable to his body. While still checking the grass, he held onto the invisible platform with one hand while walking around it and inspecting it with his other hand. He also moved an arm above the invisible platform trying to find a means of support from above. He found nothing. Then on hands and knees, the man crawled underneath the invisible platform and found no support of any kind. He returned to his feet.

Totally befuddled, the man determined the invisible platform was just there, suspended in mid-air. During his inspection, the man judged the invisible platform to be approximately seven feet long, forty inches wide and thirty inches high.

As the man backed away from what had been his former bed, he marveled at its total invisibility, and the fact it seemed to be suspended, unsupported in mid-air. While he thought there must be a rational explanation, for the present, he had no idea what that might be. He did, however, feel the invisible platform was significant and might provide important clues about this strange place and what his involvement might be.

But with the landscape being what it was, how would he ever find it again if he moved around the area much except by accidentally walking into it. Glancing around, something caught his eye that was lying under a nearby bush. On closer inspection, he found it to be a glistening green rock about the size of a melon. When he retrieved it, the man was surprised by its lightness. Walking carefully, he located the invisible platform and placed the glistening green rock in its approximate center. The man thought if he didn't wander far, he should be able to locate the invisible platform with ease.

The man walked about midway between the invisible platform and the rocky path that was the beginning of the way into the Great Valley. He thought about all he had seen when he temporally acquired the incredible and unexplained zoom vision. He was certain the Great Valley was not a place he would ever want to visit and hoped the kind of wildlife he had seen was restricted to that area only and not his location at the upper reaches.

As the man contemplated all that had transpired, he thought that his theory about finding himself alone and unprotected as an intentional act by someone was not plausible. He was now thinking that he was in some way connected to this strange place. He could remember the hospital room, then awakening on the invisible platform. Perhaps he had somehow made his way from the hospital room to the invisible platform unassisted and without being seen. If so, when he was discovered missing, a search would take place. In fact, it could already be in process.

The man looked at the sky, hoping to see a drone, helicopter or low flying plane, but saw nothing. The man thought it was strange that he did not see the sun as he was scanning the sky. A lot of time had transpired since he had awakened. He thought it must be close to midday and from his vantage point he could see much of the sky, but the sun was not visible.

The man turned his thoughts to the coming night. What if rescue didn't happen before then? The thought of spending the night alone and without shelter was terrifying. While the temperature seemed to be perfect for the moment, he knew that could change rapidly after nightfall. And what about the animals he had seen? Were there any such creatures here, in the upper reaches of the Great Valley. If rescue didn't come, the man foresaw a long, wet, miserable night that he might not survive.

The man searched the pockets of his walking shorts and shirt, hoping to find some matches, but found none. While he knew nothing about outdoor survival, he knew he had to at least try to provide himself protection. While the man had no tools to build a shelter or any way of starting a fire, he thought he would search for dead limbs lying about, carry them to the invisible platform, and stack them against and around the sides, teepee style. Then he would break small living branches from the trees and place them over the dead wood. He would leave himself an opening to crawl through, then pull a live broken branch behind him to block the opening. The man thought that should keep him dry from the dewfall, and maybe even a sudden rainstorm, which he thought must occur frequently considering the lushness of the vegetation. The man thought, while the crude shelter would offer hardly any protection from harmful animals, it might act as camouflage and prevent him from being noticed if any happened by. At least, the man thought, he had a plan.

Walking carefully, lest he injure a foot, the man marveled at the softness of the grass. He approached a nearby group of trees and searched the ground for fallen limbs. He found none. He walked from tree to tree, expecting to find dead and broken limbs that had fallen during windstorms. But the ground was clear of limbs and debris. There was nothing but the lush, dark green grass, which the man was finding to be even more comforting. As he walked along, he frequently scanned the sky, looking for the hoped-for rescue. The man also continued his search for the sun. There was not a wisp of a cloud, the daylight was very bright, he knew the day was quickly passing and he had yet to catch a glimpse of it.

The man soon grew weary of his search for dead limbs. There were none.

He then turned his attention to small, living branches. He grabbed hold of one with both hands, and twisted it back and forth, thinking it would splinter and easily break. This proved to not be the case, for no matter how much he twisted and turned, the branch would not break, and when he released it, the branch immediately returned to its original shape. After several tries with more branches, with the same results, in frustration, he gave up.

The man suddenly had the feeling that he should return to the invisible platform, for he felt it would soon be nightfall. He didn't understand how he knew this, it seemed to be an instinctual feeling. He turned and looked for the glistening green rock, and realize he had wandered farther from the invisible platform than he had intended. He had been drawn to various bushes, trees and groups of flowers that he found to be exceptional in their beauty. Due to his aimless wandering, he was now completely disoriented.

A sudden urge prompted the man to walk to the top of a small rise. From there, he spotted a many-colored tree he had previously inspected. After making his way to the tree, he again had an inner feeling about which direction he should take. Soon, to his great relief, the man stood looking at the glistening green rock that lie on the invisible platform. He felt something inside had directed his actions, allowing him to find his way. It was like a voice from within, barely audible, but proving to be very beneficial.

As he had previously done, the man walked about midway between the invisible platform and the rocky path. He sat, and thought about how he had failed miserably in his quest to build a crude shelter. The thought then occurred that he might climb one of the nearby trees, and secure himself the best he could in the unlikely event he dozed from time to time. But the man thought he would probably end up falling from the tree causing himself a serious injury. And besides, any predator that might take notice should not have a problem plucking him from a tree.

As the man sat, he once more thought about the fact that even though the sky was perfectly clear, he had not seen the sun. And, he realized he had nothing to eat or drink the entire day. Once during the day, out of curiosity, he had thought about sampling some of the abundant fruit but was fearful it might prove to be harmful. Other than that, he hadn't even thought about food or drink, and even though he had been very active, felt just fine. Also, the man realized he had no need to care for normal body functions, which he thought, could be attributed to the fact of no food or drink.

As the man contemplated these things, the daylight suddenly dimmed. In an instant, the brightness went from full-light to perhaps half-light. Then, after a few moments, it seemed as if someone was turning a dimmer switch to a lower position, for the daylight went steadily lower to almost darkness. It was not complete darkness, for the outlines of surrounding trees and bushes could be seen. Suddenly all became quiet. The man had grown accustomed to the constant activity of the birds and small animals that surrounded him. He found the silence to be deafening.

Confused about what had happened, the man started to stand. The method of the event was indeed a mystery, but nightfall was now upon him, and the man thought sitting underneath the invisible platform might at least provide him some protection. But, before he could fully rise, a weariness began to overcome him, and he sank back to the ground. Not understanding what was happening, the man tried to rise again, but could not. He was feeling a strong desire to sleep. The lush grass beneath him, and the air surrounding his body, seemed to radiate a comforting warmth. He thought he would rest a few moments and then make his way to the invisible platform.

The man slept. The man dreamt. In his dream, he saw lava slowly flowing down the side of a mountain. He watched in fascination as the lava advanced. Suddenly, a brick wall appeared in the lava path effectively blocking its downward flow. Thus restricted, the lava flow was divided into two separate streams at the brick wall's base. One stream flowed one direction, one stream flowed the other until the two streams reached the end of the brick wall. Then, each lava stream continued its downward flow, each effectively divided from the other.

The man then found his presence to be at the top of the brick wall. Lying on top of the wall, he saw a sheet of paper. There were three words written on the sheet of paper. The man squinted as he peered at the sheet of paper while trying to read the three words. But no matter how he tried, the letters were blurred and ran together, and he could not read what was written. Then the dream left the man, and he fell into a deep restful sleep.

The man awoke. He felt secure, warm, and comfortable as he stretched luxuriously. Then he remembered where he was. He quickly surveyed his surroundings and saw the outlined trees and bushes in the almost darkness. The thought occurred that he should now be cold, wet, stiff and in general miserable after spending a night in the open with nothing but grass as his bed. But, as it turned out, he found it to be quite the opposite. Except for a strange dream, he remembered nothing. And thankfully, it appeared that no roaming predator had been in the vicinity.

As the man sat up and started to contemplate his next move, the almost darkness suddenly turned to half-light, and then in a reversal of the previous evening, grew steadily to full light. He could hear the beginning of rustling of wildlife. He instantly looked at the sky both for the sun and a sign for the hoped for rescue but saw nothing.

As the man looked upward, the sky appeared to be full of dark dots that seemed to be slowly drifting toward the ground. His first thought was that a very large swarm of gnats were descending onto the entire area. But as he sat transfixed, a soft gentle mist, reddish in color, covered his body. The mist was pleasing to his skin and caused a feeling of comfort, along with an anxiousness to begin the new day. The man remembered the dream he had before awakening on the invisible platform. Perhaps it had not been a dream.

The man saw that the strange mist was being absorbed by his body. This frightened him, for he had no idea what the strange substance could be. Half running, half crawling, he made his way to the invisible platform and sat beneath it in order to shield himself from the soft gentle mist. But, to his astonishment, the mist appeared to fall directly through the glistening green rock and the invisible platform.

From his position, the man raised his hand to feel the underside of the invisible platform and found it to be dry. Then, upon inspecting himself, he found his walking shorts and shirt were dry also, but his skin underneath his clothing, along with the rest of his body, was covered with the mist. He could think of no plausible explanation for this. After a few moments more, the soft gentle mist stopped falling and the surrounding area started to come alive with sounds of activity.

The man crawled from beneath the invisible platform and surveyed the surrounding area. It seemed all things had been covered with the mist which was quickly disappearing as it was absorbed. He found his own body was now almost completely dry. But, the effect of the soft gentle mist remained, and instead of feeling dread because of his current situation, he found himself eagerly anticipating this new day. As the man stood by the invisible platform, contemplating what his immediate actions should be, he felt his hunch about being connected to this place was correct. And it was imperative he discover in what way. He thought there had to be someone who could explain this to him.

And he thought there had to be a way in and out of the upper reaches of the Great Valley.

The man let his gaze fall across the Great Valley. To venture there would only be going deeper into the mystery, and he had no desire or intention of ever going there. The opposite direction, away from the Great Valley would be the logical way. Perhaps a wall or fence protected the entrance and exit area.

Probably there would be guards and other methods of surveillance, and hopefully, an avenue to find answers. He thought the location he desired may not be far from his current position. He found himself leaning toward the theory he had somehow wandered to the invisible platform by his own initiative.

The man started his venture and walked upward, and away from the Great Valley. He was determined he would not allow himself to become pre-occupied by interesting and unusual sights but would continue on at a steady pace. He planned to judge his distance and time spent walking with the intention of returning to the invisible platform before the almost darkness if he was not successful in finding an exit way. The man felt a need to be near the invisible platform as long as he was in the upper reaches of the Great Valley. As he walked, he pondered all that had happened. He continued to glance at the sky for signs of rescue and the elusive sun. He felt if a rescue party arrived at the invisible platform, after seeing the glistening green rock on top, the rescuers would realize he had been there and would continue their search, hopefully in the general direction he had gone.

The man walked by a large bush and was surprised to see a deer. Its neck stretched as it plucked fruit from the higher branches. The deer glanced at the man as he passed, but showed no signs of fear. A little farther, and he saw two deer grazing on the lush grass. They also showed no concern as he walked by, and the man felt if he wanted, he could reach out and touch them. He felt their reaction to him was an indication it was rare for humans to be present, and they had not learned to fear man.

As the man continued on, he realized he had completely forgotten about searching for dangers that might be hidden beneath the grass. He had as yet to see any foreign objects and there were moments when he walked across bare rocky areas that were completely void of grass and experienced no discomfort to his feet. It felt as if he was still walking through the grass. The man observed an abundance of animal life. Some were familiar to him, some were not. All seemed unconcerned of his presence, and none seemed to be of a kind that would pose a threat. He hoped he was correct in assuming the dangerous animals inhabited only the Great Valley.

The day was passing quickly, and the man saw nothing to indicate he might be close to discovering a way out of the upper reaches. As he approached a rise, the man decided he would walk to its top, and if he saw nothing of interest would attempt to retrace his steps and return to the invisible platform. He thought he might even find a rescue party waiting there. When the man reached the top of the rise, he stood gazing down toward a stream that flowed through a gentle, rolling landscape. Trees and bushes bordered both sides of the stream, and patches of flowers grew profusely. Butterflies fluttered about performing an aerial dance. The man spotted what appeared to be an otter swimming downstream. As he stood watching, the otter dove beneath the water.

The man started to walk toward the stream, but the voice from within informed him he should start his return to the invisible platform. Not wanting the almost darkness to overtake him, the man turned from the stream. He was quickly learning the importance of the whispered information. And once again, it proved to be true, for by obeying the gentle urging, the man had no problem retracing his steps, and soon stood before the invisible platform and the glistening green rock.

During the day, the man had constantly thought about the mysteries he had witnessed and thought he had developed credible theories to explain them. The invisible platform was supported by a magnetic field. The zoom vision he attributed to a satellite whose camera was trained on the Great Valley. The man thought he had, in some way, activated an invisible screen while sitting on and grasping the sides of the invisible platform. The sun was not visible because it had in some way been blocked and thus allowed only beneficial rays as well as light through without the sun itself being seen. The man attributed this to both the amazing colors and lushness of the foliage and grass. The blocking of the sun was apparently a two-step procedure which would account for the two stages of light before the almost darkness and again for the return of daylight. The soft gentle mist was probably caused by a low flying satellite that released the substance at a specified time each morning. The mist would contribute to the nourishment of the plant and animal life, and probably, along with the blocking of the sun, the color scheme as well.

And who was behind all of this? That was indeed an intriguing mystery. While it was possible the government was responsible, after considering all the amazing events he had witnessed and experienced, the man thought it most likely, space aliens. That would also explain the man-like creatures he had seen walking along the outer edge of the Big Forest. They were probably a subspecies with some degree of intelligence, and their function was close up inspection of the results of scientific experiments in the dangerous Great Valley. The purpose of the invisible platform was for technical observation from a safe distance by using the zoom feature. If it were not space aliens and turned out to be the government, what about these man-like creatures? The man thought the answer to that would be Big Foot. The man wondered where he fit in with all of this. His theory was that he possessed some sort of special skill that made him valuable to the ones in control of the Great Valley. But, while performing this skill, an accident occurred, perhaps exposing him to a dangerous substance that caused him to experience delirium and he being admitted to a secret, special care unit for treatment. Somehow, he must have wandered off without being observed, and then made his way to the invisible platform. Though they seemed incredible, the man thought his theories were plausible.

As he had done the previous evening, the man walked about halfway between the invisible platform and the rocky path that led into the Great Valley. He sank to the ground and wondered what the almost darkness would bring.

Would he be as fortunate as the night before? The man marveled that he had gone two full days without nourishment or water. As active as he had been, he should by now be famished and very thirsty. But, when he had discovered the stream, instead of running to it as a man tortured by thirst would, he had calmly walked away and returned to the invisible platform, and he realized he still had no need to care for his normal body functions.

The man realized this could not continue. No matter if his lack of interest in food and water was due to the soft gentle mist or some other phenomena, he knew he must provide nourishment and water for his body, or he would not survive. He determined, baring a calamity during the almost darkness, that after the daylight returned, he would venture to the stream, drink a small amount of water, and sample the fruit from the trees and bushes that were in the stream's vicinity. The man thought if the fruit was edible, the juice alone might sustain his need for fluids until rescue came. He was wary about drinking water from the stream for he feared it might contain harmful bacteria. The man was certain since he already knew the stream's location, he would have no problem returning to the invisible platform before the almost darkness.

Then, as had happened the previous evening, the daylight went to half light. As before, the half-light went steadily down to the almost darkness. The man didn't attempt to seek refuge under the invisible platform. He had fared well the night before in the open. He could feel the need to sleep overcoming his body. As quietness fell, the man lie on the soft grass and felt its comforting warmth. Soon he was asleep and the dream came. As the night before, he saw lava flowing down a mountainside. A brick wall stood before the lava, blocking its flow. The lava ran into the base of the brick wall which created two streams of lava. Part of the flow went one direction, part the other direction until they reached the end of the wall. Then, the two streams of lava took their own separate course down the mountainside. The man found his presence at the top of the brick wall, and he examined the sheet of paper that lie there. But, no matter how he tried, he could not see the words written on the sheet of paper. The dream left him, and a deep and restful sleep fell over him.

The man awoke. He was in comfort. As he lie in the soft warm grass, he thought about his dream. It was the same dream he'd had the night before. He found it odd but could think of no explanation. The half-light came, then grew to full light. The man could hear the surrounding area start to come alive. The soft gentle mist started to fall. The man lie still as he felt the mist fall across his body. It passed through his clothing as if he wore nothing while leaving his clothing completely dry. The man started to feel the sensation caused by the soft gentle mist, and wondered if the mist was beneficial or detrimental, but knew it didn't matter, for there was no way of escaping it. Shortly after the mist stopped falling, the sounds of activity increased.

The man stood and walked to the invisible platform. After absorbing the mist, he was anxious to begin the day. He would follow his plan and start immediately for the stream. He looked at the glistening green rock and again thought it would indicate his presence to anyone who might see it. He turned away and started toward the stream. The man was struck by the beauty that surrounded him but did not delay to inspect or admire. He wanted time to explore the area around the stream before returning to the invisible platform. The man thought the seemingly perfect conditions he had experienced the two previous nights might in some way be caused by the invisible platform, and he was fearful of facing the almost darkness away from it.

According to the whispered information he received, it was late morning when the man stood gazing down at the stream. He did not hesitate but walked hurriedly to the stream's edge. He estimated the stream to be about thirty feet in width. The crystal-clear water that flowed before him appeared to be no more than waist-deep. The man realized he had no way of knowing about the safety of the water but was determined to drink a small amount.

His next decision was, how? Should he cup his hands and lower them to gather the water, or simply lower his head and drink directly from the stream? The man knelt and started to lower his head, but abruptly stopped when he saw his reflection in the water. Something was different about his appearance, but he didn't know what. Puzzled, the man gazed at himself for several moments before he lowered his head to the water. Just before his lips touched the stream's water, the man was taken aback, for he could feel the water flow to his lips and into his mouth. It seemed the only effort required by the man was to swallow. He found the taste to be both delicious and refreshing, so much so that he forgot about his intention to drink only a small amount. The man allowed the water to flow into his mouth for several moments, not because of thirst, but because of the pleasure of the taste.

When he finished drinking, the man started to rise. He stopped when he saw a bush on the opposite side of the stream start to shake. To his horror, as he watched the movement of the bush, a large grizzly bear walked from behind it and sauntered to the stream, stopping directly opposite the man. Every fiber within the man shouted for him to rise, turn and flee. He wanted to put as much distance between himself and the bear as quickly as possible. But he thought it would be folly. The bear as yet had not seen him, and the man thought if he remained perfectly still it may not even notice him.

The grizzly looked across the water directly at the man. It cocked its massive head in apparent confusion. Then, the bear slowly lowered its head to the water. As the man watched, he saw the bear was drinking from the stream in the same way he had, for the man could tell the water was flowing on its own into the bear's mouth.

When the bear finished drinking, it reared up and stood on its hind feet.

The man's heart skipped a beat. He knew if the bear attacked, it would be across the stream in seconds. There would be no way of escaping. But, to the man's surprise and relief, the bear, still standing, walked back to the bush and started to eat its fruit, then dropped to all fours and after looking once more in the man's direction, the bear walked downstream for perhaps fifty feet. The bear crossed the stream and started walking in the general direction of the invisible platform.

After he saw the direction the bear had taken, the man quickly abandoned his plan about returning to the invisible platform. He knew this would mean he'd spend the almost darkness at a different location. This troubled him, for he didn't know what type of conditions to expect away from the invisible platform. Would the grass continue to be dry and warm, and would he sleep safely through the almost darkness, or did these conditions exist only in the vicinity of the invisible platform? But it seemed the man had no choice in the matter, for the last thing he wanted was another encounter with the grizzly bear.

The man walked several feet upstream, then veered away from the flowing water. He did not want to chance another encounter with a thirsty bear. As he walked along, he envisioned a bear behind every tree and two behind every bush. Thankfully, none materialized, and as the afternoon passed, the man again found himself appreciating the serene beauty of his surroundings. As the man approached a grove of trees, the voice from within whispered that almost darkness would arrive soon. He knew his moment of reckoning was near, and he would discover if conditions were the same throughout the upper reaches of the Great Valley.

The man decided to enter the grove of trees to wait for the almost darkness. It shouldn't matter if he was within the tree grove or on its border, for hopefully the prevailing conditions would see him safely through the almost darkness regardless of his location. Fortunately, he found conditions to be similar to the past two evenings, and the man soon found himself drifting off to sleep.

The man dreamt his dream, then fell into his deep restful sleep.

The man awoke. He thought about the strange recurring dream.

Although puzzled about the dream, he was thankful he had once again survived the almost darkness unscathed. Then as he expected, the half-light appeared and then steadily increased to full light. He was by now accustomed to the sequence of events, and he lie waiting for the soft gentle mist. Even though the man was still concerned the mist might prove to be harmful, there was no denying the exuberance it caused. In fact, he found himself looking forward to the occurrence.

After the soft gentle mist had fallen, even though he still did not feel hunger, the man stood and pulled a piece of fruit from a low hanging branch. After taking a small bite, the effect was immediate, and he found himself savoring the flavor of the fruit. The bear encounter the day before had caused him to delay eating any fruit. His main concern had been to put distance between himself and the bear. But now that he had finally tasted it, the man was finding it difficult to stop eating. He sampled a variety of the fruit and found all to be delicious.

The man heard the chattering of a squirrel. Looking high into the tree he was standing beneath, he saw a red squirrel apparently scolding him for snatching the fruit from the tree. The man smiled as he looked at the squirrel. He had not realized there had been such close company during the almost darkness. After eating some more of the fruit, the man thought it was time to continue on. He was now at the farthest point from the invisible platform he had ever been and saw no reason to return. He had faired quite well during the almost darkness and did not feel as strong of a need to be near the invisible platform. There was still the possibility of encountering a bear. The man thought his best option would be to continue going away from the Great Valley. He was certain doing so would eventually lead him to the way out of the upper reaches.

As he prepared to start, the man looked at the sky. He still had hope of rescue, but it was starting to fade. He knew it was futile to search for the sun, for it was hidden, and only its effect, not the sun itself could be seen. The man walked away from the grove of trees and across an area of mostly grass.

Something soft and furry ran by him brushing the side of his leg as it passed. He saw it was the squirrel that had been in the tree foliage above him as he slept, and had watched and scolded him as he walked about sampling the different kinds of fruit.

The squirrel ran about ten feet ahead of the man, then turned and sat as it watched the man approach. He thought this was strange behavior on the part of the squirrel, but continued walking for he expected the squirrel to move. But to the man's surprise, the squirrel held its position. The man started to walk around the squirrel, but the squirrel nimbly moved with the man and continued to block his path. The man turned around and walked in the opposite direction. His plan was to walk several feet away from the squirrel, then circle around and continue on. But, before the man had taken many steps, the squirrel ran ahead of the man and once again sat and watched his approach.

The man started to feel alarm about the squirrel's actions. Perhaps the fruit or the soft gentle mist in some way affected the animals causing them, at times, to become aggressive. While this was only a small squirrel, a bite, or even a scratch could prove to be deadly if infection set in, especially without aide of any kind available.

Without thinking, the man bent and leaned toward the squirrel. He extended his hand toward the small rodent's nose. The man suddenly realized he was instinctually following directions from the voice from within. The squirrel moved forward and sniffed the man's extended fingers. The man dropped to one knee and very slowly moved his hand to the squirrel's head. He gently rubbed with two fingers in a small circular motion. The squirrel closed its eyes, and it was obvious to the man that it was thoroughly enjoying his attention. Knowing he was putting himself in a vulnerable position, the man sat, and soon the squirrel was lying against his leg as the man gently stroked its head and back. After several moments, the man stood and started walking the direction he had intended to go. He glanced down and saw the squirrel walking beside his feet. The man smiled and thought it would be nice to have some company.

The two traveled throughout the day stopping from time to time to eat from the fruit trees and bushes. While the man still did not feel hunger, he wanted the nutrition and fluids for his body. And the fruit seemed to become more delicious with each bite. The animals they encountered were all of a gentle nature, none that would pose a threat to man or squirrel. As the time grew near for the almost darkness, the two stopped in an area containing several trees. But instead of climbing one for the night as the man expected, the squirrel was lying close to his leg. This reinforced what the man had started to think, which was all the animals slept during the almost darkness. Therefore, the squirrel had no reason to fear that a predator might be in the area. This added to the degree of comfort and security the man felt in regard to the almost darkness.

When the man awoke the next morning the squirrel was still lying nearby. He had the same dream and then experienced the same restful sleep after the normal course of events that lead to the almost darkness. He was beginning to think that the recurring dream was to be a normal part of the almost darkness. Soon after the falling of the soft gentle mist, the man and squirrel ate from the fruit trees that surrounded them. Then, they continued on the journey that was leading the man farther away from the Great Valley.

About midmorning, the man saw movement directly ahead. When he was able to clearly see the brownish colored animal, he saw that it was a bobcat walking in their direction. When the bobcat saw them, it stopped. It stood, looking their direction, as it intently surveyed them.

The man felt he was too large for the bobcat to consider him as prey, and felt no concern. But, as he stood admiring the animal for its beauty, he glanced down at his little buddy, the squirrel who had also spotted the bobcat, and thought that could be an entirely different matter. While the man was no animal expert, he was certain the bobcat would consider the squirrel to be a tasty treat. However, they were in an area that contained several trees, and he expected the squirrel to quickly climb one for safety. The man thought it would be difficult for a bobcat to catch a nimble squirrel within the branches of a tree, and was certain his little buddy would be fine.

Therefore, the man was quite surprised and watched in horror when instead of scurrying up a tree as he had expected, the squirrel ran directly toward the bobcat. He could think of no rational explanation for the squirrel to do such a foolish thing and thought he was about to see a disaster unfold before his eyes. But horror turned to amazement when the squirrel ran to the bobcat. The two briefly touched noses, and the bobcat extended a playful paw toward the squirrel. Shortly after, the man's amazement returned to horror, for the squirrel ran in the direction of the man followed closely by the bobcat. The man was taken by surprise and could do nothing but watch as the pair approached. The squirrel moved to the side and watched, seemly unconcerned, as the bobcat stood before the man. The man's situation had changed dramatically, for while the bobcat was not a large animal, it was capable of inflicting serious injury.

Once more, the voice from within impelled the man to act. Even though he thought it to be foolish, he extended his hand toward the bobcat. The bobcat investigated the man's hand, then allowed him to gently rub its head. Still following the whispered instructions, and realizing it might prove to be folly, the man sat. To his relief, the bobcat lie beside him, and the man felt what began as curiosity on the part of the bobcat was quickly turning to affection. As the man stroked the bobcat, they were joined by the squirrel. The man had already forgiven his little buddy for leading the bobcat to him.

The three of them roamed throughout the upper reaches of the Great Valley. No way out could be found, and as the days passed, the man rarely looked with hope for rescue, or out of habit for the sun. The bobcat never hunted for food and when it did eat, seemed to be quite content with fruit from the bushes and trees. Whenever they came upon a source of water, they drank more for the delicious taste than necessity, for it seemed the abundant fruit provided their need for fluids. Each night the man dreamed his dream then fell into the deep restful sleep.

No animals were encountered that would be considered threatening to the man. Many, however, should have been natural enemies of the bobcat and squirrel. But no fear or hostility was exhibited between the animals and peace reigned. The man had come to the opinion that the experiments being conducted within the Great Valley and upper reaches of the valley were to provide an abundance of healthy food for the world's population. But now, after observing the interactions between the different species of animals, he opined to himself that this might include research on a method of altering the destructive nature of man.

One afternoon, the three of them came upon a relatively flat area that was mostly dominated by grass and bushes. They walked deeper into the area, and the man realized the fruit was of a kind he had not yet tasted. He sampled the fruit and found it to be very pleasing. The man thought an afternoon in the area would be time well spent. He quickly changed his mind, for as the man looked several feet ahead, he saw a grizzly bear walking from behind a bush. The bear vanished as it walked between another group of bushes. As the man stared in disbelief at what he had seen, another grizzly came into view. This bear also was lost from sight as it followed the path of the first.

Not wishing to test his theory about peaceful interactions between the different species of animals, the man thought it best to leave this place as quickly as possible. But, before he could turn, the man felt a slight pressure on the nape of his neck. He froze in place, for he knew that a grizzly bear stood directly behind him. The man thought there were two courses of action available to him. He could stand where he was, and wait for powerful jaws to crush his skull or a mighty paw to smash the side of his head, or he could turn and watch as powerful jaws crushed his skull, or a mighty paw smashed the side of his head. The man chose the latter.

He turned and stood face to face with the grizzly. The voice from within told him to proceed as he had with the squirrel and the bobcat. The man extended his hand toward the bear. The grizzly sniffed the man's hand, then not satisfied, moved its head close to the man's face for closer inspection. The man stood ridged as he fought the impulse to turn and flee. After what seemed to be an eternity the bear pulled away. The man breathed a huge sigh of relief, and he gently rubbed the bear's head. The bear sat, then lie on its side. The man sat beside the bear and petted its back. The man heard sounds of movement. When he turned his head, he saw the two bears he had previously seen walking his way. Soon, the man was surrounded by the huge grizzly bears interacting with them in ways he never thought possible. The squirrel and bobcat lie nearby, seemingly unconcerned with the bears' presence.

After the encounter with the bears, the days passed without incident, as the man, squirrel and bobcat continued to roam throughout the upper reaches of the Great Valley. The man felt a restlessness growing within. The thought of his finding a way out of the upper reaches, or of rescue finding him, had completely faded. He found himself filled with an overcoming compulsion that he was in search of something. While he had no idea what the object of his search was, the man was certain he would recognize it whenever it was found. And the man knew, whatever it might prove to be, the object of his search would not be found in the upper reaches of the Great Valley, but only in the depths of the Great Valley itself. The man felt this endeavor was something he must do alone, and would soon have to part with the squirrel and bobcat.

While his two companions seemed to realize they would soon be going separate ways, the strong feeling of compatibility between the three remained intact. And most comforting to the man was the overwhelming feeling this was not going to be goodbye. The squirrel and bobcat would always be a part of him, and the man was certain they were destined to meet again. The day soon came when the man started out alone. After walking several feet, he turned and saw the two watching. He felt as if they were, in some way, conveying to him that all was well between them. Smiling, he turned and continued walking.

The man's intention was to return to the invisible platform that held the glistening green rock. He would spend a period of time in the general area, while he planned his venture into the Great Valley. Several days had passed since his encounter with the bear at the stream, and he had traveled many miles. However, he was not worried about locating the invisible platform. The man suddenly had a brief memory flashback: soft laughter, a voice telling him he would get lost if he attempted to walk around a block by himself. Taken aback by this, the man found himself conceding that was probably a true statement. But he now had the voice from within to rely on and was confident in its ability to guide him to his destination. As the man walked along, he dwelt on the memory flashback, but it had been fleeting and barely discernable, existing only on the farthest outskirts of his memory.

After several days of travel, the man knew he was nearing his destination. He had recognized several landmarks, and the voice from within informed him it would be but a short period of time before he once again stood in the presence of the mysterious invisible platform. Only a few steps more, and he would see the glistening green rock. The man stopped short and looked in amazement not at the glistening green rock as he had expected, but rather a house. The house was not large, it was a little house. He noticed it had the appearance of not being fully complete.

The man stood for several moments as he searched for activity, but saw none. He thought it would be both foolish and dangerous to approach the little house without first knowing who might be present and for what reason. Was it possible rescue had arrived after all, or could the existence of the little house point to a nefarious plot? The man thought it best to stay hidden until he determined who was present. But he received whispered information informing him the little house was vacant.

The man circled to the front of the little house which faced the Great Valley. There was an opening for a door, but no door was present. To the side of the door opening was an opening for a window, but no window was in place. The man walked through the door opening into the first room. An oversized chair sat before the window opening which offered a view of the Great Valley. He stood a moment, then he walked through another door opening into the second room.

This room had one window opening. A small couch sat against a wall. The invisible platform was also in the second room, but the glistening green rock had been replaced by another object. The man walked to the invisible platform and looked down at the object that rested on it. He stood for several thoughtful moments, then lightly touched the object and gently moved his fingers over it. Then, he turned and entered the third and last room. The third room had a window opening as well and contained a midsize bed and a small chair.

The little house was of supreme construction with every corner and every angle of a precise dimension. The roof was flat, and the entire structure made of a type of wood the man had never seen. He estimated the dimensions of the little house to be approximately thirty-four feet long by thirteen feet wide. He thought it was indeed an impressive structure. The man was aware the almost darkness would soon arrive. He found himself torn between the desire to sleep outside in the open or within the boundaries of the little house. He had come to the conclusion that the soft gentle mist was beneficial, but he was certain the little house would not restrict it from entering. The man returned to the first room. He sat in the oversized chair and gazed through the window opening that overlooked the Great Valley.

After the almost darkness arrived, the man succumbed to sleep. He dreamt his dream, but this night it contained more than before. After reaching the ends of the brick wall, and continuing down the mountainside as two separate streams, the man watched entranced as the two streams of lava flowed between nooks and crannies, cracks, and crevices before merging together and continuing once more as one. As the man watched the merger take place, he felt a sensual warmth overtake him that he felt to the very core of his being. The man then experienced the part of his dream concerned with the sheet of paper and the three words that were written on it. He then entered the period of deep restful sleep.

The man awoke. He sat in the oversized chair and waited for the two changes that led to full light. As the man expected, when the soft gentle mist fell it was not inhibited from passing through the roof of the little house. The man remembered his dream, along with the addition to it, and felt the warm sensuality of the moment. He had originally planned to remain in the area of the invisible platform for a period of time before venturing into the Great Valley. However, since the discovery of the little house, he saw no reason to delay. It seemed one mystery led to another, and he was anxious to begin his search. The man knew that if successful, he could be provided with the answers he had been looking for.

Part II

The Great Valley

Shortly after the falling of the soft gentle mist, the man started down the rocky trail that was the beginning of the way into the depths of the Great Valley. After walking several feet, he followed the trail as it curved to his left. The man turned and looked in the direction of the little house. He found it could not be seen from this vantage point for his field of vision was obstructed by an array of trees, bushes and boulders. The man continued on, and soon the trail wound back the other direction. Once more the little house was visible. The rocky trail then led steadily downward and soon the little house could no longer be seen.

The man wondered how the animals that inhabited the Great Valley would react to his presence. Hopefully, they would in the same way as those he had encountered within the upper reaches, this being curiosity that quickly turned into genuine affection. He had but a short period of time before knowing. The man spotted them several feet ahead, bison, their large shaggy heads lowered as they stood grazing. The man, who had determined not to avoid any animal he came upon, continued to walk toward them. It was a herd of around fifty buffalo. As the distance between them narrowed, the huge animals noticed him and stood watching his approach.

A large bull lowered his head and walked toward the man. Not wavering in his resolve, the man continued on directly to the buffalo. He patted the side of the animal and was rewarded by several satisfied grunts. Soon, the man found himself surrounded by the entire herd. He walked slowly among them, speaking softly as he did, to their obvious delight, petting and patting the heads and sides of the beasts. The man was aware the animals were careful not to press against him and gave him the space he needed to move freely among them. The man spent several enjoyable moments interacting with the buffalo. The days passed and the man continued his search. He encountered various kinds of animals. Some were herd dwelling, others in small numbers or alone. He was amazed at the large diversity of animals that roamed the Great Valley. Many should have been separated by large masses of land or bodies of water. But they coexisted within the boundaries of the Great Valley living in harmony and relying solely on the grasses of the fields and the fruit and foliage from the trees and bushes for sustenance.

For the man, each day held new adventure. He was grateful for the interactions with the animals, and continually amazed with the seemingly unending variety of trees and bushes as well as the beautiful colors and the tastiness of the fruit that grew among their branches. The landscape was scattered with streams, ponds and small lakes that abounded with waterfowl, and there were occasional waterfalls glimmering in the brightness of the day as the water cascaded down to waiting pools below.

Each night after the almost darkness arrived the man dreamt his dream, then slept the deep restful sleep. The soft gentle mist made its morning appearance invigorating the man and prepared him for the arrival of the new day. The sun was never visible, but the man's ways were clear and bright. Rain never occurred, but water was plentiful, the man supposed from reserves that lay deep below the earth. His facial hair never grew, and normal body functions, for whatever reason, were not required. He thought this abnormity might be attributed to the soft gentle mist and diet of exotic fruit. The object of the man's search was often on his mind. He felt a growing anticipation at the prospect of discovering the reason for his odyssey, but at the same time, did not feel disappointment that, as yet, his searching had not ended. Since awakening on the invisible platform, the need for rush and hurry had steadily decreased, and the voice from within, on occasion, whispered to the man that time was not important.

On this day, the man found himself walking across a large expanse of mostly flatland. He had been walking across the flatland for several days. On several occasions, he had come upon herds of deer and antelope, and once entered an area that contained a pride of lions that roamed at will among a large herd of antelope. Neither species seemed concerned or interested in the presence of the other. The lions ate berries from low growing bushes as they walked among the grazing antelope. When he had first started this long walk, the forest he was approaching appeared to be no more than a tiny speck that spread across the horizon. But now, the man was struck by the sheer massiveness of the forest. To his left and right as far as he could see, the trees grew, and the man had no doubt that when the plain he had been walking across yielded to the forest, the trees continued for hundreds of square miles.

The man walked to the forest's edge and scanned the area within his vision range. The trees appeared to be a uniform height of around thirty feet. The bark of the trees was smooth and greyish white in color. The foliage was of a variety of colors with branches heavy with fruit. Fruit growing bushes ranging from four to six feet in height grew in groups of three or four. The forest floor was covered with thick green grass similar to that he had walked on while crossing the plain.

The man was impressed by the neatness and cleanness of the surrounding area. He saw no broken or fallen limbs, no toppled trees, no tangles of vines or bush nor prickly briars. All was order. The man walked into the forest for closer inspection and found the limbs and branches of the trees to be too high for sampling their fruit. However, the bushes were another matter, and soon he was walking through the soft grass, plucking and eating the bush fruit which he found to be delicious.

The man walked deeper into the forest. He found himself among the man-like creatures before he realized. In fact, at first, he thought the trees were moving, for the hair that covered their bodies was identical in color to the bark of the trees. He judged them to average approximately seven feet in height. They were in a group of around thirty and moved slowly along as they plucked fruit from the bushes or reached high above their heads for the fruit that was within their reach. The man's first impression of the huge, hairy creatures was Wild Things.

The Wild Things noticed him, and one by one stopped their foraging and stood gazing in his direction. The man, not wishing to display a conspicuous manner, pretended not to notice and continued inspecting the bushes for the choicest pieces of fruit. He was hoping that by ignoring their puzzled stares and acting as if he belonged, the Wild Things would simply accept him and allow him to remain among them.

As the man stood before a fruit-laden bush, he felt a slight pressure upon his upper back. He turned his head to see the reason for this and saw that a large hairy hand as big as a baseball mitt gently held on to his shoulder. The man turned around an looked up, then looked up higher still into the searching eyes of a Wild Thing with a height of at least nine feet. The man's feeling of utter dwarfishness as he stood before the magnificent fellow prompted the title of Mr. Big.

Mr. Big looked up, reached high into the overhead branches, and plucked a piece of splendid-looking fruit. He held the fruit toward the man apparently as a goodwill offering. Not wishing to offend, the man quickly accepted and bit into the fruit. He did not need to exhibit feigned enthusiasm, for the fruit contained a special sweetness he, as yet, had not tasted. Upon seeing the man's pleasure, Mr. Big smiled. The big fellow turned toward the onlooking Wild Things and spread his long arms wide, indicating to the man he was welcome to commune with the group and to partake in the offerings of the forest. The man stood and watched as Mr. Big and the Wild Things resumed their normal activities. He gratefully, and somewhat humbled, followed suit.

Each day the man traveled with Mr. Big and the Wild Things deeper into the forest. The encounters that occurred with the many different species of animals were always peaceful. Conditions were the same as the man had experienced elsewhere, and he continued to have his nightly dream. Mr. Big and the Wild Things displayed a high degree of intelligence, along with a relationship that was bonding. They participated in a variety of game-like activities. Favorites seemed to be a version of tag, running races and a game that combined keep away while attempting to advance a single, round, basketball-sized tree-fruit between two makeshift goalposts. All was in good fun, and when Mr. Big participated in the events, none could run faster or jump higher than he. While no vocal sound ever came forth from the Wild Things, in some unexplained way they seemed to have a form of communication. At first, the man thought it might be through sign language, but after close observation, he was forced to abandon that theory. The man was leaning toward the intriguing theory the Wild Things communicated through telepathy.

The deeper into the forest the band of travelers walked, the larger and taller the trees became. The man also took note the trees were becoming more uniform in size and shape. During this period, other small groups of Wild Things were encountered. These quickly blended into Mr. Big's group, and the original band of around thirty rapidly grew in size. Soon after, the appearance of the trees became identical. They had grown massive in circumference, with no means of determining their measurable height.

The limbs that grew from the trunks of the trees were truly amazing.

Starting approximately ten feet above the ground, and continuing at ten feet intervals, a circle of twelve limbs, each limb averaging about thirty inches in width, grew horizontally at perfect right angles from the massive tree trunks. The ends of these limbs grew to the ends of the limbs of adjacent trees, effectively creating a continuous level walkway throughout the different levels of the trees. This system of growth continued as far upward as the man could see. It appeared as if small branches grew along the edges of the big limbs that offered a variety of fruit.

The man observed several Wild Things climb into the massive trees. They ventured to different levels, then walked along the pathways the limbs provided. This surprised him, for he had not seen a Wild Thing climb into a tree before this, and had thought they must prefer the ground over climbing. But now, some were climbing to heights that exceeded his vision's range. As the man watched the spectacle in amazement, he knew even if he had the ability, he would never have the desire to climb the giant trees. He was quite content to keep his feet on the solid ground. The man felt a light tap on his shoulder.

The man turned and found himself looking upward into the eyes of Mr. Big.

The big fellow looked above his head while pointing and moving a long finger which indicated a large area of the upper forest. The man's first thought was that Mr. Big was commenting on the activity of the Wild Things that was taking place high above their heads. The man responded with a smile and an affirmative shake of his head. Mr. Big studied the man, then with what the man took to be an almost apologetic expression on his face, pointed his finger at the man, then upward. The man was starting to feel he didn't like the direction the conversation was headed. He smiled politely, shook his head no, then started to turn away.

Before he took a step, Mr. Big placed his big hands under the man's armpits, then lifted him and gently placed him in a sitting position on one of the lowest level limbs. In an instant, Mr. Big climbed to the limb and stood over the man.

After a smile and a reassuring pat on the head, Mr. Big lifted the man and placed him under his arm as if he was no more than a rag doll. Using his free arm, Mr. Big started to climb. His hold on the man was firm yet gentle, and the man felt no discomfort as Mr. Big made his way toward the tops of the trees. The man tightly closed his eyes. While he could not imagine why Mr. Big was taking this course of action, the man knew the big fellow would never intentionally harm him and felt no ill will toward Mr. Big.

Finally, the man chanced a quick look. As he looked downward and saw nothing but a dizzying maze of limbs and realized how far away the ground had become, he thought it best to again close his eyes and wait until Mr. Big reached his intended destination and then examine his surroundings. The man's hope was Mr. Big wanted him to see and sample exotic fruit that grew at the uppermost heights of the giant trees, and then would return him to the forest floor. But something caused the man to look upward, and as he did, he gasped at what was before his eyes. As he looked in amazement, the man knew he was looking at the last level of limbs. At this level, each limb grew about five feet outward from the trunk in the normal manner. At this point, the limbs' width increased dramatically. The result of this caused each limb to grow against and to become part of its two neighboring limbs. This resulted in the making of a solid and apparently mostly flat surface. Whispered information informed him the surface continued for miles.

The man knew Mr. Big was about to climb through the opening they were nearing, and what was above would be revealed. As Mr. Big approached the opening, the man thought about and marveled at the brightness of the daylight. While he had theorized that harmful rays from the sun had been blocked and the sun could not be seen due to some type of cloaking device, the sun was still there. The light came from the sun, and even without this upper floor, the part of the forest that existed underneath the giant trees should have received little light because of the trees' massive size. But the forest floor had been as well-lit as an open field. Now, with the discovery of the solid upper floor, the man wondered why all beneath was not complete darkness. Except for the small openings against the trunks of the trees, all was covered with the upper floor and the light from the sun should have been effectively blocked. However, this mystery would have to be pondered another time, for Mr.· Big was about to climb through the opening.

After climbing through the opening, Mr. Big walked some distance from it before releasing the man from his grasp. The man stood in awe at what greeted him. Mr. Big's upstairs flower garden was an excellent description the man thought for flowers grew profusely. The sweet fragrancy of them was carried by a gentle breeze. Their colors were mirrored and in striking contrast to a large number of butterflies that fluttered about. Several small trees and bushes also grew and were visited by colorful birds and small animals. The grass grew golden, and the sunless, cloudless sky seemed an even deeper blue. Mr. Big stood before the man, a smile on his face. Then, as he had done on their first encounter, the big fellow spread his arms wide, in effect indicating to the man he was also welcome here in the enchanted land high above the forest floor. As the man stood alongside Mr. Big, something white flashed in front of him and landed upon his shoulder. He craned his head to the side and saw that a small grapefruit-sized animal of some sort rested upon him. The man extended his arm across his body and found that the little animal was as soft as cotton. The man quickly decided the small cotton ball monkey would be welcome to ride upon his shoulder whenever it wanted. He looked again at Mr. Big and saw that he too, had acquired not one but two of the soft, cuddly little animals. It was apparent that Mr. Big was delighted with this development as he gently petted the two little cotton ball monkeys with one of his big fingers. Then, with a wave of his hand and a smile upon his face, Mr. Big joined in with the other Wild Things that were roaming about.

Mr. Big's upstairs flower garden was overflowing with enchantment. Most of the animals and birds the man encountered were of a kind that he had never before seen. His favorite remained the small cotton ball monkeys. It was rare when two or three of the little animals were not riding upon his back or shoulders. As the days passed, and the Wild Things and man continued to roam within the upstairs flower garden, the man saw an ever-changing landscape. Small streams filled with colorful fish were abundant, as were quiet, peaceful pools of water that sparkled in the bright daylight. The man's whispered information indicated that water deep below the forest traveled through the root system of the giant trees, sustaining the trees as well as providing water for the upper level of the forest. Trees, bushes and other plant life flourished, but the dominating growth was flowers. The Wild Things had continued to grow in number, and they maintained their normal activity. It was evident to the man their opinion of Mr. Big was one of respect and admiration, and there was no doubt the Wild Things considered him their leader. There were no changes in the man's daily activities, and he considered it normal during the almost darkness to dream his dream before entering the deep restful sleep.

One morning, shortly after the soft gentle mist had fallen, a faint, peculiar sound caught the man's ear. The sound was barely audible, and after determining its origin, the man started walking in the sound's direction. The man noticed several Wild Things were also going toward the strange sound. As the man drew closer, he realized the source of what he was hearing was the sound of voices joined together in song. This had a surrealistic effect upon the man. He had not heard another's voice since awakening on the invisible platform. The man realized the lyrics were of a strange tongue he could not understand, but felt them to have a strong drawing effect. The man crossed a small stream, walked around several bushes, then stopped short at what lay before him. On a grassy mound with a scattering of flowers stood Mr. Big, surrounded by eleven of his Wild Things. All were singing the hypnotic lyrics that held the large number of spectators spellbindingly fascinated. Entranced, the man sat and listened, and though he could not understand the meaning of the words, time stood still as Mr. Big and his accompanying Wild Things sang their beautiful song.

When it was over, the large audience of Wild Things slowly disappeared. The man sat and pondered all he had seen and heard. His theory that visitors from another planet were the cause of all that occurred within the Great Valley, and the fact they were able to keep it hidden, pointed to something only an advanced civilization could accomplish. Since he had seen no actual physical evidence of this alien super race, the man wondered if some disaster had befallen them, and now all that remained were the Wild Things whose duties had been on-site observation. As the man remembered the strange mesmerizing language of Mr. Big and the Wild Things as they stood singing, it was not difficult to believe it was the language of another world.

As the man considered this empirical evidence, his role in all that had transpired was still a mystery. However, the yearning to resume his search was flaring inside of him, and the man realized the time had come to depart from the Big Forest. Soon after, Mr. Big made an appearance, and a mutual understanding flowed between the two. The man and Mr. Big walked to an opening at a nearby tree trunk, and the two began the journey to return to the forest floor. The man felt at ease as Mr. Big climbed downward, and kept his eyes open and enjoyed the ever-changing beauty that passed before him. Once on the ground, the two stood and intently stared into the other's eyes. As it had been with the squirrel and the bobcat, the man felt no sadness, for the whispering from within informed him this was not goodbye. He and Mr. Big would meet again. It appeared the big fellow felt the same, for after the man received a gentle hug, a soft pat on the head, and a big smile, Mr. Big returned to the tree trunk and began to make his way back to the upper floor of the forest. The man watched until the big fellow was out of sight. He was alone again, deep within the interior of the Big Forest, but the man knew what was to be his next destination, and also knew the voice from within would direct his steps.

After a journey of several days, the man once again stood in awe at what lay before him. As he had recognized the mysterious wonderment of the Big Forest upon approaching it, so too did he recognize the profound greatness of the majestic Large Water. That its boundaries were large the man did not doubt, and that it was tremendous in depth he was certain. The man walked to the shoreline and stood looking over the water. Neither wave nor ripple did he see. All was smooth as glass. He knelt, scooped some water into his hand, and placed it to his lips. Fresh, and although tasting somewhat differently from the water of the streams and lakes, was very good. The man walked slowly into the water. It was crystal clear with a soft sandy bottom. He walked several feet before the water approached his knees. The man walked farther into the water and began to notice small, colorful fish darting about. The small fish glimmered in the bright daylight.

The water's depth increased very slowly, and the man walked several feet more before it approached his waist. He smiled as a small, bright red turtle swam by paddling its way toward deeper water. The man began to notice different varieties of aquatic plant life. Schools of small fish swam around and within the plants, feeding on what appeared to be clusters of very tiny berries. Another several feet of walking and the downward slant became a rapid decline. The water soon was to the man's neck. The waters beauty called out to him, and the man pushed forward with a strong rhythmic stroke. As he swam, he peered downward into the clear water in an effort to see what was below. The man saw midsize fish swimming about, but nothing more before his vision was obscured by the water's depth.

Suddenly, the voice from within informed the man that it was time to return to the land for the almost darkness would soon arrive. As he treaded water, the man turned and looked toward the shore. He found he had been so entranced by the beauty and splendor of the Large Water, that he was shocked at the distance between himself and the shoreline. This gave the man cause for thought. What if he found himself in a compromising situation, but was prevented from reaching a safe location before the almost darkness arrived.

Would he be able to stave off the sleep that accompanied the almost darkness until he reached a safe area, or would he succumb to the sleep and suffer whatever consequence the situation called for? The man was not worried though, for the voice from within always gave him an adequate amount of time to reach a safe area before the almost darkness fell. Then he saw the fin.

The huge fish came up from the deep water behind the man. Its dorsal fin sliced through the water as it passed on the man's right at a distance of twenty feet. The man continued to tread water as he turned with the fish. It maintained its distance and continued to circle the man. Finally, the fish stopped directly between the man and the shore he desperately wanted to reach. Because of the water, the man could see but a poor reflection of the fish. It appeared to the man that the mouth of the fish was constantly opening then closing as it held its position. The man was certain he could see rolls of teeth as he looked into the wide gaping mouth. The man considered his predicament and felt anger that he had allowed himself to be caught in such a situation. He should have considered the possibility of danger lurking in a body of water such as this. While he had successfully coexisted with all the creatures previously encountered, he was now in a completely different environment and he was dealing with a fish.

The mammoth before him slowly started to sink into the water. The man did the same, for he feared the fish would attack from below. He was surprised at how easily he controlled himself under the water, and at least, for as long as he could remain so, would have a clear view of his adversary. The man estimated the depth of the water to be around forty feet, and he and the fish were at the midway point. As the mouth of the fish continued its movements, the man was surprised to see there were not rows of razor-sharp teeth that would be useful for biting and tearing, but rather short clusters of teeth most likely used for grinding aquatic vegetation. Also, now that the man could more clearly see the fish, he saw that the lower portion of his mouth was in the shape of a scoop. However, the man had no doubt the huge fish could easily swallow him with a gulp, then swim off in search of dessert.

After several moments of studying each other, the fish moved slowly toward the man, its big mouth constantly working. The man had no choice but to hold his position. When the fish was a distance of about six feet, it sank deeper into the water. The man pushed upward with his arms and hands so he too would go deeper and remain on the same level as the fish. The two remained in the face-off for several moments more before the fish once again swam toward the man. Seconds before he thought the huge gaping mouth was about to engulf him, the fish swerved, its big mouth looming as it swam past on the right side of the man while keeping its body close. Instinctually, the man turned toward the fish while extending his arm. He touched the side of the fish and let his hand slide against the soft skin as the fish swam by. The fish swam several feet before turning, and it again swam closely past the man who once more let his hand slide against the side of the fish. Again, the fish turned swam within a few feet of the man and stopped. The man started rubbing the side of the fish just inches from the gaping mouth. For the man, time seemed to stand still.

The man was struck as if hit by lightning. How could he have been so foolish, so mesmerized by the fish that he forgot the need to breathe? Air, he must have air. The man looked upward. The twenty-five feet of water between himself and the surface seemed more like two-hundred. In a panic, he frantically flailed his arms, while wondering if he could reach the surface before he was forced to draw water into his lungs. But then he stopped. The voice from within informed him all was well. There was no need for a mad rush upwards toward the water's surface and life-giving air. But that was impossible, the voice from within lied. His brain was close to death, and it too, lied, as it tried to compensate for what it realized was about to happen. His delayed reaction had probably cost him his life. Once more, his eyes opened wide in panic, the man started to swim upward.

Then, he again stayed his frantic movements. He had been submerged much too long to still be conscious. If not already dead, he should be at the point of no hope of living. But he was fine. He had automatically stopped breathing when he had gone below the water, and the man realized he would not breathe again until he surfaced and he was fine. As the man pondered this startling revelation, the daylight dimmed. The big fish slowly sank and rested upon the sandy bottom. The man did likewise and sat a few feet from the fish. When the half-light changed to almost darkness, the man lie on his side. The sand was soft against his body, and the water that surrounded him provided a sense of security. As the man was drifting towards sleep, he realized his forearm had fallen partially within the mouth of the fish. He smiled as he felt the huge mouth gently closed periodically against his skin. The man dreamt his dream before falling into the deep, restful sleep.

When the man awoke, his position had shifted during the night, and his arm was no longer within the mouth of the fish. He awaited the daylight and wondered about the soft gentle mist. Could the mist possibly penetrate the surface of the water and have any plausible effect. When the daylight arrived, the man looked upward and saw the sky was filling with the soft gentle mist. As the tiny droplets fell into the water, tiny nano explosions were created that propelled the droplets at tremendous speed. The man was certain the droplets reached, clung to, and were absorbed by every living creature and all plant life that existed under the surface of the Large Water, including the deepest areas, due to the propelling force created by the nano explosions.

With the soft gentle mist, came the feeling of wellbeing along with an excitement of beginning the coming day. The man was eager to swim over the deeper water and observe as far as his range of vision would allow. The huge fish made a slight movement and was almost against the man. The man found himself looking into a big eye. A silent communication passed between the two. With a push of his feet, the man propelled himself to the back of the fish. The fish began to swim toward the deeper water as the man held on to the dorsal fin while leaning to the side in an effort to penetrate the water's depth.

Suddenly, the man regained the zoom vision he had obtained for a short period while sitting upon the invisible platform. As the fish continued its way over the deep water, the man found himself looking several miles downward. Between his position and the bottom, the man saw creatures as large as buildings and as small as ants. There were creatures that swam through the water, and creatures that walked or crawled along the bottom.

The man observed a stunning array of life and a myriad of colors. Some creatures exhibited astonishing flashing lights as they swam or walked along. Everywhere the man looked, all was peace, all was order.

As the man observed and contemplated all that he had seen, he wondered if it would be possible to descend to the bottom of the Large Water. Would his body withstand the tremendous pressure and temperature change at such depths? The man knew the answer was yes. He and his huge friend could explore wherever they desired under any circumstances without experiencing any adverse results. But now was not the time, and time was not a problem. He knew the right moment would arrive for further exploration. The man's zoom vision left. The big fish turned and swam in the direction of the distant shoreline. As the man reflected on all that had occurred, a deep sense of finality overwhelmed him. He found the implication to be enormous. The fish carried the man as far as possible without beaching itself. The man slid down and patted his friend's side. As with the squirrel, bobcat and Mr. Big, the man knew he and the fish would meet again. This was not goodbye.

The man continued to the shore. He turned and stared across the water. He was now ready to admit to himself what he knew to be true. He had known for some time, but couldn't bring himself to face the reality. He had searched for every possible answer while denying the obvious. There was no other conclusion to be drawn. The man was certain when he had awakened on the invisible platform, he had awakened to the supernatural. He was in the realm of the spiritual. As he gazed out over the water, the big fish jumped, then gracefully turned in midair and returned to the water with barely a splash. Then, with a flip of his tail, the big fish was gone.

The man, in deep thought, continued looking at the spot where the fish had jumped. He now knew what was different about himself whenever he saw his reflection. A brief flashback had revealed he died a feeble old man confined to the boundaries of his bed. But when he had awakened on the invisible platform, he had awakened as he had been in his physical prime, and as that he would remain. The man realized that the zoom vision had nothing to do with the invisible platform. Although he as yet did not understand how it worked, he now knew it was a spiritual attribute, and the moment would arrive when he would be able to activate it whenever he desired. The fruit he ate and the water he drank did not sustain his life. He would be fine without either. They were a reflection of his physical existence to be enjoyed whenever he desired. The little house was symbolic of both his physical and spiritual existence. Why should he need more than an opening for a doorway, and why should the window openings contain windowpanes? He did not need protection from the elements, for conditions were perfect. And who would threaten? What if a bear wandered inside? That would be wonderful. Or what if Mr. Big and some of his Wild Things came by for a visit? That would be better still. Perhaps the Wild Things would sing their hypnotic lyrics, and perhaps he would be able to understand the meaning of their beautiful language.

The man turned and looked in the direction of the little house. It was many miles away and would take several days of walking to reach. The man knew there was a way to be there in an instant, but didn't understand how.

But that didn't matter. It wasn't the time for the little house. For now, he would continue his search, a search for an answer that when the moment was right would be revealed. The man turned and walked alongside the Large Water, and wondered what the coming days would bring.

After several days of travel through the coastland, the man arrived at the river that flowed through the center of the Great Valley and emptied into the Large Water. His plan was to cross the river and then proceed in a meandering way in the general direction of the little house. The river was wide and flowed swiftly, but after his underwater experience with the big fish, the man had no problem in crossing. Early one morning a few days after he crossed the river, the man walked across a flat grassland area and came upon a herd of around one hundred hartebeests. As he approached the hartebeests, the large antelope started running. This troubled the man, for never before within the Great Valley had any animal shown fear. Then he realized it wasn't his presence that had caused the antelope to run, but rather the soft gentle mist that had fallen not long before. The antelope were energized and running for the sheer pleasure. The man happened upon them at the start of their run. As he stood and watched, the man could feel the excitement of the hartebeests. They moved across the grassland as one, as if guided by an invisible hand. The herd of antelope made a wide circle, then headed back toward their starting point. As the animals drew close, the man realized they were not stopping, but would continue their run. He braced himself as the animals ran by, some brushing against him as they ran past.

The man turned and continued to watch the antelope. He found himself wishing he could be part of the herd and run along with and alongside of the antelope to share their exuberance as they raced across the grassland. Then, once more they turned and ran toward him and still, they showed no sign of slowing.

The man thought he would experience being part of the herd if only for a short period of time. He turned his back toward the antelope and took the standing start position. The man turned his head and watched as the running animals grew near, and at what he judged to be the right moment, with a yell, started to run.

The lead antelopes were soon abreast of the man, and he was certain he would quickly be left far behind. But, to his surprise, the man found himself maintaining the pace of the antelope.

The man's arms and legs worked as pistons as he raced across the grassland with rhythmic flow. He felt as one with the herd and knew exactly what the movements of the animals would be. After returning once more to the starting place of their run, the antelope and the man stopped. The man rubbed and stroked the animals as he walked among them. A brief flashback in memory caused him to remember a moment when he had run with others like himself. But at the end of that run, he had stood with hands on hips in a bent position while attempting to regain his breath. Yet now, even though he had run much farther and faster, he was no more winded than he would have been strolling leisurely through a field of flowers. The man wondered what other changes in strength and endurance might occur as he advanced in his spiritual life.

The man remained in the general vicinity of the river for several days. At times, he walked along its banks, at other times he veered several miles away as he explored different areas of the Great Valley, interacted with the abundance of wildlife, and continued his search. One afternoon he discovered a small canyon and found its beauty and splendor to be breathtaking. He ventured into the canyon and came upon a waterfall which was the beginning of a stream that wound its way through the canyon. The man followed the stream for he thought he might come upon a bear or perhaps two that were enjoying the fruit that grew in abundance upon the trees and bushes that grew along the banks of the stream. About fifty feet ahead, the man saw that the stream made a sharp curve to the left. At that point, about five feet from the stream, lie a big black boulder. The man saw that something was lying upon the big black boulder. He could not tell what the object was, but it was yellow in color and seemed foreign, out of place. His curiosity aroused, the man quickened his pace in order to more quickly examine the yellow object. Then, as the man approached the sharp bend in the stream and the big black boulder that lie nearby, his search ended.

The woman had just stepped from the water. She was nude, and the man found her beauty to be overwhelming. At the sharp bend in the stream, the water swirled, which created a refreshing and exuberating sensation as well as attracting a multitude of colorful fish. The woman had entered the stream to enjoy the effects of the water and to examine the beautiful fish that swam around her. She gently stroked the fish as they swam by and nudged her ankles, legs and thighs. The woman started to reach for the simple yellow dress she had laid on the big black boulder before entering the water. She seemed to feel the man's presence. The woman turned toward him. Their eyes met, and there was a brief moment of confused déjà vu. The woman showed no fear of the man, nor did she show any embarrassment at the state of her undress. With a pondering expression upon her face, the woman turned away and retrieved her dress. After placing it over her head, she pulled it down her wet body. Then, with the beauty and grace of a panther, the woman leaped upon the big black boulder and sat facing the man.

The man joined the woman upon the big black boulder. He had no idea what she might have experienced or to what degree her spiritual advancement might be. They talked, as two people who had inadvertently met and found each other interesting enough to start and then continue a conversation. The beauty of the canyon was exceptional, the fish that swam nearby were spectacular and the fruit and berries that grew along the winding stream splendid in taste. Aimless but enjoyable conversation that they continued throughout the afternoon.
The fact that they would leave together, and stay together was a given. There was no reason for the subject to be discussed. The man felt the need to return to the little house. He had no doubt it was important to do so, but the voice from within informed him that he and the woman should pursue an explorative route as they made the journey to the little house. The man was then certain he and the woman would arrive at the little house at the correct moment.

During the following days as they traveled along together, the woman told her story. She had awakened early one morning lying on the ground. While she had felt no discomfort, she was confused and very frightened. The two-step process of the almost darkness becoming daylight, and the falling of the soft gentle mist shortly after added to her fear. But after the event of the soft gentle mist, her fears were abated. The woman started to explore her surroundings and heard the barking of a dog. Bounding toward her, its tail wagging, she saw a beautiful dog of mixed breed that the woman believed was mostly St. Bernard. She fell to her knees and flung her arms around the dog as she held it close, and tightly hugged its neck. The man smiled at this account. What better companion and protector could the woman have had than a faithful dog.

The first evening she was frightened by the process that led to the almost darkness. But the presence of the dog comforted her, and she slept well, waking refreshed with the dog lying closely against her. The woman quickly developed a deep feeling of trust toward the dog and was grateful she was no longer alone. She thought it strange the dog never hunted for food but rather seemed content with the berries that grew upon the smaller bushes. The woman found the fruit and berries to be delicious, and as the man thought, they would provide fluids during periods water was not available. The woman made no mention of reoccurring dreams as the man was experiencing. By the description of her surroundings, the man was certain she had awakened that first morning much farther within the Great Valley than he had.

The animals the woman and dog encountered exhibited no fear. She soon found she could easily approach deer and small animals and pet and fondle them at will. The dog was good-natured, and it sniffed noses to greet new acquaintances, or lay quietly and watched as the woman interacted with the animals. The woman was thankful that, as yet, no animal had made an appearance that should be considered dangerous. However, that changed one day as she and the dog were walking across a flat grassy area. Several feet ahead a grizzly bear stood, watching as she and the dog approached. The dog stiffened when it saw the bear, then immediately ran toward the large animal. The frightened woman thought she would have an opportunity to escape while the dog held the bear's interest, and she turned to flee. But she found she could not abandon her faithful friend. The woman ran toward the dog and the bear. She hoped the barking dog, along with her shouting and waving her arms, would frighten the bear, and it would leave. But her resolve turned to horror when instead of barking and growling as she had expected, the dog touched noses with the bear, then ran directly toward the woman followed closely by the large grizzly bear. Taken completely by surprise, the woman could do nothing but watch helplessly as the two approached.

The dog ran to the woman, licked her hand, then moved a few feet to her side and sat watching as the bear approached. Unable to move, the woman stood ridged with her hands tightly clenched. When the bear's snout approached her face, she wished the bear would be quick in taking her life and end the horror.

The woman wanted to close her eyes and wait for the end, but somehow found the courage to keep them open. She could hear the bear sniffing as its nose lightly touched her face. But, when the woman thought she could stand no more, the bear sighed and gently rolled over onto its side. In disbelief, the woman realized the bear meant her no harm. Sobbing and shaking she fell to her knees and buried her face in the bear's thick fur. When the dog walked over and sat against her, she stroked it with one hand and the bear with the other. The man's pity he felt toward the situation the woman had been in turned into respect for the courage she had shown, as he remembered his first close up encounter with a bear. The woman had shown loyalty and bravery, and his admiration for her grew.

The woman, dog and bear remained together and continued their wandering. Many of the animals they started to encounter were, like the bear, of a more ferocious nature. The woman was not concerned whenever this occurred, for after the encounter with the bear, she had quickly learned she had nothing to fear from any creature within the Great Valley. As the days passed, the woman, as the man had, experienced a restlessness. While she didn't understand what it might be, she felt there was something she needed to do. And, like the man, felt she must do it alone. To the man's interest, the woman recounted to him that when the moment came for her to go her separate way, she felt no sadness. There had been the feeling within her that the dog and bear would always be a part of her, and that the three of them would again interact together. After going her own way, the woman had spent several days aimlessly wandering before she ventured into the canyon and eventually encountered the man.

While many of the woman's experiences were similar to his own, the man realized there were also differences. But one thing was evident, it had been meant for them to find each other. As the days continued to pass, the man and woman grew closely together, and a strong, unbreakable bond soon developed between the two. They held hands laughing like children as they continued to explore the wonders of the Great Valley and delighted in the ever-changing splendor. The two swam together in the lakes that dotted the landscape and lie closely together during the almost darkness, each appreciating the closeness of the other. But what the man had come to believe was his heaven, had also partly become his hell, for while being identical to the physical in appearance, the spiritual was not capable of physical lovemaking. Because of this, their love for each other did not seem complete. The woman understood the man's frustration and felt it herself. Their solace was they had found each other and were experiencing their spiritual existence together. The thought of it being any other way was unbearable.

As the familiarness between them continued to grow, the man told the woman about the little house and some of the mysteries associated with it. And, when he felt the moments were right, he recounted his experiences within the Big Forest and the Large Water. The woman, mostly in silence, listened intently to the man's narratives, but at times could not contain her excitement. While she agreed the little house was a puzzle and was anxious to see it, she trusted the man's judgment about the timing of their arrival. She was enthusiastic about visiting the Big Forest and seeing Mr. Big and the fantastic upstairs flower garden. The woman's interest was evident when the man spoke of Mr. Big and a small gathering of Wild Things singing the mysterious but beautiful lyrics. And her eyes sparkled with delight as the man told her of the little cotton ball monkeys.

Though he knew the woman had experienced many extraordinary events before his arrival at the big black boulder, and that she understood they were in a spiritual realm, the man wondered if she would doubt his account of the Large Water. But the woman gazed at him with trusting eyes as he told his story of the big fish and the fact that he had been able to survive while underneath the water's surface. Not only did she believe the man without question, but indicated an underwater adventure was something she would pursue as soon as the opportunity presented itself. The man was grateful for the woman's trust, but as he stared into her eyes, and remembered the fear he had at first felt he wondered what her reaction would be when she made her first attempt to survive, unassisted, while below the water's surface.

Once, as they were strolling along, the woman stepped aside and leaned against a mid-sized boulder. There was a strange expression upon her face, and it was apparent she was deep in thought. When the man asked if something was wrong, the woman had a strange question for him. She asked the man which side of his chest contained his heart. Stunned, the man simply stared at the woman.

The woman then told him that shortly after awakening in the Great Valley, she had discovered her heartbeat was stronger than normal. And, she had been alarmed to discover her heart was not in its normal location but was on the opposite side of her chest. This had been weighing upon her mind, and the woman had decided to ask for the man's opinion. The fact was, the man had noticed his own heartbeat was stronger than before, not excessively so, but definitely more pronounced. However, his heart was in its normal location, slightly to the left of the center of his chest. With a sigh, the woman took hold of the man's hand and placed it upon her chest in what would be the normal location of the heart. The man felt nothing. She then moved his hand to the other side of her chest, slightly to the right of center. Unmistakably, the man felt a strong, healthy heartbeat. To be certain about himself, the man placed his hand upon his own chest. His heart was beating strongly, and its location was as it should be, slightly to the left of the center of his chest. The man pondered this strange revelation about the woman, and could only conclude it was related to some strange spiritual attribute. The two sat in silence for several moments.

Late one afternoon, the man and woman walked down a grass-covered slope that ended at a narrow ledge. Twenty feet below the ledge, lie the water of a clear sparkling lake. As the woman stared into the lake, the man had a feeling of apprehension. Before he had related to her his account of the Large Water and big fish, whenever they had swum together, he had shown a feigned need to surface at regular intervals in order to replenish his lungs. But since the woman now knew it was possible to survive without air while under water, it was only natural that she would want to experience and obtain this fantastic spiritual attribute for herself. And the man knew that was exactly what she now planned on doing. As he stood watching, the woman removed her yellow dress and laid it neatly upon the ledge. Then, without hesitation, she made a graceful dive into the water. The man quickly removed his walking shorts and shirt and entered the water moments behind the woman. He immediately saw the water was very deep.

The woman was several feet below him and had come to a stop. She remained motionless as the man swam slowly toward her. When the man drew near, she looked beyond him, toward the water's surface. Then, stricken with what the man knew was uncontrollable panic, the woman swam upward in a frantic effort to reach the surface as quickly as possible. The man watched as the woman broke the surface and remained in place while treading water. He swam toward the woman, his intention to console her and give solace over the failed effort. But, before he reached her, the woman sank beneath the surface and once more swam downward.

The man watched in amazement as she swam past with a determined look upon her face. As he watched her descent, he realized the woman had swum beyond the point of no return. If it turned out the woman needed air, she could not possibly reach the surface in time to replenish her lungs. This did not bode well with the man. What if she did not have the ability to survive underneath the water? As he started swimming toward the woman, he found the implication of this thought very troubling. However, his fear was laid to rest when he reached her and saw the smile upon her face. As he again remembered trying to cope with his own fear, the man once more was struck by the courage the woman had shown. They celebrated her triumph with a smile and a hug. It was apparent to the man that the woman was in no hurry to leave the water but wanted to experience her newfound ability to the fullest. They soon found themselves exploring the tranquil beauty of the lake's underwater world. While the man was certain there was a method of communicating in an environment such as this, he thought it was a quality the two of them would acquire as their spiritual existence progressed.

When the time grew near for the almost darkness, the woman indicated her desire for them to remain underwater. They lie close together on a soft bed of aquatic moss. As always, the man dreamt his dream before falling into the deep restful sleep. When the daylight returned, they watched in awe as the droplets from the soft gentle mist turned into tiny nano explosions after striking the water surface. The man knew the droplets found their way to every living creature and all plant life within the lake. Shortly after the soft gentle mist, the man and woman returned to the water's surface. They were both elated with the fact the woman had conquered her fear, and the two of them would now be able to explore together the underwater beauty that existed within the Great Valley.

The man sat and watched the woman. The two of them had been leisurely walking along the banks of a stream when a beaver emerged from the water. The woman immediately started playing with the animal. The beaver lie on its back, its webbed hind feet rapidly moving as if it was attempting to tread air as the woman rubbed and fondled its stomach. The man smiled as he watched their antics. The voice from within had informed the man that he and the woman were about halfway to the little house, and they should continue on as they had been doing. The man's confidence in the whispered information he received had continued to grow. There was a sense of comfort related to the voice, along with an authoritative nature the man had come to believe should not be ignored. He rose and joined in with the interaction between the woman and the beaver.

Afterward, they continued on, lingering at times to enjoy special areas of beauty, and to sample the large assortment of fruits and berries that grew along the stream.

When the time drew near for the almost darkness the two chose an area not far from the stream to spend the night. As always, they lie close together as they awaited the almost darkness. After it arrived, the man started drifting to sleep. His dream occurred. He watched as the lava stream flowed into the brick wall then split into two streams. One stream moved one direction; the other stream moved the opposite direction along the base of the wall. As always, when the two streams traveled the length of the brick wall and were no longer restricted, they again flowed downward as two separate streams before finally meeting and merging together and then continuing on as one smooth uniform lava flow. The man felt a warm sensuality as he watched the two streams of lava merge.

The man then found his presence at the top of the brick wall. The sheet of paper with the three words lie below him on the wall's top. But this night something was different, for another object was lying atop of the brick wall alongside the sheet of paper. The man looked, then recoiled in shock and surprise. Glasses! Even though the man had acute spiritual vision whenever he dreamt, he could not read the three words written on the sheet of paper. Instinctively, the man knew the glasses would allow him to read the three words. His hands shook as he reached for the glasses. He was fearful of what he was about to do, but could not stop himself. Slowly he raised the glasses to his face and put them in place. The man looked at the sheet of paper. The three words leaped at him. A name, a name he had forgotten, a name that had remained in the world of the physical. The name was his own and seeing it opened a storehouse of memories. The man awoke.

Instantly, a rush of imagery passed before him. A rapid regression that moved so quickly he could not comprehend the blur that was before him. The regression slowed, and the man realized he was seeing events that were moving backward in time. There was a ceasing of the occurrence. The man found himself observing a mother holding a newborn baby close to her breast. Nearby, a proud beaming father looked on. The man realized he was the baby, and he was observing events shortly after his birth. Again, the process started, but now the speed was normal. The man found himself viewing progressive imagery. He saw a multitude of events that happened during his physical lifetime. Happenings with parents, siblings, peers, occurrences at school, in sports, college, the beginning of his professional career, and the woman.

He then saw himself as a young man, standing before his mother. She handed an object to him and told him it was the Treasure of Truth. She had said to follow its guidance and his way forward would be clear. The object was the same that now was lying upon the invisible platform within the little house. As the man watched this event between his mother and himself, words from the item she had given him surged through his mind. "A man's steps are directed by the Lord. How then can anyone understand his own way?" (Proverbs 20:24 NIV) It was a profound question, but the answer was simple. The man now realized it was an impossibility to understand one's own way. In the physical world, he had become separated from God, and he failed to focus on the spiritual unseen qualities which led to faith, hope and love, but rather had focused on self, and focusing on self had proven to be his downfall. He had become obsessed with the lies of the world and had sought happiness and satisfaction through fame, power, wealth and pleasures of the flesh. Between himself and the woman, there had been anger, lies, betrayal, and counter betrayal. Attempts at reconciliation had proven to be non-availing. Separation, sadness, loneliness and a deep unyielding regret for words not said, deeds not done had been all that remained. The man lie silent flooded by these emotions. His entire being ached as he revisited those terrible moments.

At that moment, it was revealed to the man that the woman was his soulmate. Each had been created for the other to travel together throughout eternity and to share each step of their spiritual advancement. As the man contemplated what had occurred, he wondered if his past rebellious nature would hinder his and the woman's spiritual journey. The woman moved. The man realized she too had awakened. He could hear soft sobs and knew she also had just had a similar experience as he and had come face to face with her own demons. And now as he, she knew the truth about them. The man placed his arm underneath the woman's neck, and for the first time, they lie awake during the almost darkness as they awaited the daylight. While the revelations in regard to their prior physical existence and their subsequent failings proved to have a profound, sobering effect, the two of them realized they didn't have the power to go back. Their only recourse was to move forward and rely on faith in the love they felt for each other.

The man and woman walked across a grass-covered

field. The man lingered behind in order to examine a colorful, odd-shaped rock that had caught his attention. The woman, who was several steps ahead of the man, walked slowly as she had become transfixed by several large butterflies that fluttered nearby. The man left the rock and quickened his steps. As he approached the woman, he saw she was nearing an area of waist-high grass. Within the grass, a lion lie very still, its eyes fixed on the woman. The only movement was an occasional twitching of its tail. Because of her interest in the butterflies, the woman failed to see the lion. As she grew near, the lion rose. Surprised, the woman stopped. Then with a laugh, she rushed forward and flung her arms around the lion's neck. The lion gently rolled over on its side pulling the woman with it. It then lie in obvious contentment as the woman petted and rubbed the lion's thick fur.

The man continued toward the two but stopped short as he caught movement from the side. He turned his head and saw real trouble, and it was headed his direction. Two young lions had appeared from behind a bush and were racing toward him. The man realized what was about to occur and braced himself. Still, when the pair reached him, he went down in a tangle of legs, paws, wet noses and investigating tongues. After wrestling with the two for several moments, the man heard laughter. He knew the woman was watching his predicament with glee. However, the two young lions soon tired of the man and turned their attention toward the woman. The man watched the resulting, good-natured tussling between the woman and two young lions. A lioness made an appearance.

She walked in a dignified manner and sat next to the man. He draped an arm across her back and gently fondled her fur. The lion walked over and lie on the man's opposite side. The three watched as the woman and young lions frolicked in the soft grass.

As the days passed, the man and woman wandered across hills and through dales as they continued on in the direction of the little house. The man still had his reoccurring dream of the flowing lava, but since he had been successful in reading his name and the revelations that had followed, the sheet of paper atop the brick wall was absent. While not certain of their future, each felt a sincere, unselfish concern for the other. From this they found comfort. One afternoon, the man and woman came upon an area of moss-covered ground. The softness of the moss resembled the softness of the plumage of young birds. The woman removed her dress and lie on the moss, reveling in its luxurious softness. She rose and playfully unbuttoned the man's shirt. The man removed his shirt and walking shorts. They were lying together side by side upon the bed of moss.

The strength of the woman was close to that of the man. She turned to her side and faced the man. She then reached across his body and grasped his shoulder. She pulled him with her as she again lie on her back. Taken by surprise, the man found himself atop the woman. Her eyes sparkled as she placed her hands behind the man's head and pulled him close. Then, for the first time, he tasted her kiss and found it to be sweeter than the sweetest fruit in Mr. Big's upstairs flower garden. The kiss was long, lingering, and satisfying. When the man started to raise his head, he found that he could not. He opened his eyes and found himself staring into the eyes of the woman. He saw confusion. Then, in his mind's eye, the man saw the lava from his dreams. The two streams flowed separately down the mountainside before finally finding each other, merging together, and continuing as one. As he watched the two lava streams coming together, the man's entire being was consumed by a sensual warmth, and he knew what was about to occur. The man began to feel his body slowly sinking into, merging with, and becoming a part of the woman's body.

He felt fear, fear of the unknown, fear of two becoming one resulting in the loss of identity. But the process had started, and could not be stopped. Two spiritual hearts were in perfect alignment. Electricity surged throughout when the two hearts touched. The hearts still beat as two, for they were not yet synchronized, and the man could hear the sound of both. As the merger continued, ever so slowly the beating of two hearts changed into the beating of one. The process stopped. The merger was complete, and where there had been two bodies now there was one. The body was lying still. All was quiet on the outside, but inwardly a torrential surging of emotions was occurring unlike either of them had ever imagined. Unbridled pleasures so great they led to a feeling of guilt that such ecstasy could be experienced. But then, the knowledge was given to them that the understanding of the spiritual from a physical perspective was distorted, and what they were now experiencing was the norm.

A pressure began to build, a pressure both knew would have to be relieved. A void opened before them. Then the coming apart, their essence hurled into the emptiness with tremendous speed and force. They became a whirlwind of energy as they strived to fill the emptiness of the void. Then, a gradual slowing, followed by a peaceful drifting and a sense of being one with the universe. The coming together started, the essence of the two leaving the void and returning to the body. The heart started beating. The man felt himself slowly rising upward. For several moments, their hearts beat as one, then distinctly became irregular as the process continued and the two hearts separated. Then it was over. The man rolled over and lie next to the woman. Instinctively, she raised her head allowing him to slide his arm under her neck. Neither spoke as they lie together thinking about the thing that had happened, the thing that would be theirs to share throughout eternity.

Part III
The Visitor

They were nearing the little house. As they walked up the rocky path, the man knew it would soon come into view. When they saw the little house, the Visitor was there. He appeared as he truly was, pure energy and light. The inhabitants from the surrounding area had sensed the Visitor's presence and had flocked to be near him. He seemed to glide as he moved among them obviously enjoying this small part of his creation. The man and woman walked around the curve in the rocky path, and for several moments the little house was lost from sight. When it once again came into view, the animals were gone. The appearance of the Visitor had changed to that of a man.

His hair was above his shoulders, neatly cut. His beard and mustache closely followed the contour of his face, showing meticulous care. He wore a loose-fitting white robe. Sandals were on his feet. The Visitor stood watching as the man and woman walked toward him. The man realized he and the woman were about to experience the most momentous event of their existence never to be equaled. The consequences would last throughout eternity. Words from the treasure of truth that lay on the invisible platform came to the man: “He is the image of the invisible God, the firstborn over all creation. For by him all things were created: things in heaven and on earth, visible and invisible, whether thrones or powers or rulers or authorities; all things were created by him and for him. He is before all things, and in him all things hold together.” {Colossians 1:15-17 NIV)

As they grew near, the Visitor raised a hand in greeting. They saw the scar.

The man now realized why he and the woman had been barefoot during their spiritual journey. They had been walking upon holy ground. They walked up to, stood before the Visitor, and found themselves looking into eyes of unconditional love. They worshiped him. There were tears, there was laughter. A promise was fulfilled: “Come to me, all you who are weary and burdened, and I will give you rest. Take my yoke upon you and learn from me, for I am gentle and humble in heart, and you will find rest for your souls. For my yoke is easy and my burden is light.” (Matthew 11:28-30 NIV)

All communication between them was by thought. Everything was clear and concise leaving no possibility for them to not fully understand his questions, nor for their answers to be anything but truthful. No subject was taboo, nothing set aside as forbidden or placed under a prohibition for discussion except for mysteries only God could understand. The man and woman sat at the Visitor’s feet as he taught them. All of his teachings were fully absorbed and retained.

Their questions for him were fully answered. Their wisdom, understanding, and knowledge increased many times over.

As the man and woman sat gazing at the magnificence before them, the daylight dimmed. The man knew the almost darkness would arrive soon, and he feared when he and the woman awoke the Visitor would be gone. But as the Visitor's eyes met his own, the man realized that would not happen. Not only was he now gazing at the source of light that lit this spiritual world, but also the cause of the soft gentle mist which was symbolic of the sacrificial blood that gave them life. The man knew this would not be goodbye, for that concept did not exist in the spiritual realm. The Visitor's presence would always be near, and there would be personal encounters throughout eternity. Never again would they be separated from God.

And no matter what their spiritual advancement, when they moved on and were reunited with loved ones, and conversed with angels and the saints of old, they would periodically visit the Great Valley with all its beauty and very real inhabitants they had come to love. For the gates of the Heavenly City are never closed and they would be free to come and go as they desired. All this and much more would occur at the right moments, and time didn't matter for time no longer existed.

As the man felt himself drifting into a dreamless deep restful sleep, the woman close by his side, the treasure of truth that lie on the invisible platform spoke. "Oh, the depth of the riches of the wisdom and knowledge of God! How unsearchable his judgments, and his paths beyond tracing out! Who has known the mind of the lord? Or who has been his counselor?

Who has ever given to God, that God should repay him? For from him and through him and to him are all things. To him be the glory forever! Amen." (Romans 11:33 - 36 NIV)

www.ingramcontent.com/pod-product-compliance
Lightning Source LLC
Chambersburg PA
CBHW030348100526
44592CB00010B/873
* 9 7 8 1 9 4 9 8 0 9 9 9 2 *